PIANO/VOCAL/GUITAR

CLASSIC
Eagles

"Eagles On The Border" Album Cover Painting: Beatian Yazz;
© 1974 Elektra/Asylum Records

"Hotel California"
© 1976 Elektra/Asylum/Nonesuch Records

"One Of These Nights" Album Photo by Tom Kelley Studios
Artpiece & Lettering by Boyd Elder

"Desperado" Album Photography & Lettering: Henry Diltz
© 1973 Elektra/Asylum Records for the United States
and WEA International, Inc. for the world outside of the United States

"Eagles" Album Photography: Henry Diltz
© 1972 Elektra/Asylum Records for the United States
and WEA International, Inc. for the world outside of the United States

T0050926

CONTENTS

ALREADY GONE

Words and Music by
JACK TEMPCHIN and ROBB STRANDLUND

WITCHY WOMAN

Words and Music by
BERNIE LEADON and DON HENLEY

TAKE IT TO THE LIMIT

Words and Music by
DON HENLEY, GLENN FREY
and RANDY MEISNER

THE BEST OF MY LOVE

Words and Music by
DON HENLEY, GLENN FREY
and JOHN DAVID SOUTHER

HOTEL CALIFORNIA

Words and Music by
DON HENLEY, GLENN FREY
and DON FELDER

On a dark des-ert high-way,   cool wind in my
Her mind is Tif-fa-ny twist-ed.   She got the Mer-ce-des

NEW KID IN TOWN

Words and Music by
DON HENLEY, GLENN FREY
and JOHN DAVID SOUTHER

There's talk on the street;__ it sounds so fa-mil - iar.
You look in her eyes;__ the mu - sic be-gins to play.

TAKE IT EASY

Words and Music by
JACKSON BROWNE and GLENN FREY

TEQUILA SUNRISE

Words and Music by
DON HENLEY and GLENN FREY

Take an-oth-er shot of cour-age, won-der why the right words nev-er come,_____ you just get numb.____

JAMES DEAN

Words and Music by
JACKSON BROWNE, JOHN DAVID SOUTHER,
DON HENLEY and GLENN FREY

Dean, you said it all _ so clean, _ and I know my life _ would look all right _ if I could see it on the sil - ver screen. _ We'll talk a-bout a low-down bad _ re-frig-er-a-tor, you were just too cool _ for school. _

PEACEFUL EASY FEELING

Words and Music by
JACK TEMPCHIN

LYIN' EYES

Words and Music by
DON HENLEY and GLENN FREY

DESPERADO

Words and Music by
DON HENLEY and GLENN FREY

LIFE IN THE FAST LANE

Words and Music by
DON HENLEY, GLENN FREY
and JOE WALSH

She held him up, and he held her for ran - som in the heart_
all the right peo - ple; they took all the right pills._____ They threw

_____ of the cold, cold_ cit - y. He had a
out - ra - geous par-ties; they paid heav - i - ly bills. There were

A7

nas - ty rep-u - ta - tion as a cru - el dude.__ They
lines on the mir - ror, lines on her face. She pre -

said he was ruth - less; they said he was crude.___ They had
tend - ed not to no-tice; she was caught up in the___ race.

one thing in com - mon: they were good in bed.___ She'd say,
Out ev - 'ry eve - ning un - til it was light, he was

"Fast - er, fast - er. The lights are turn-in' red."____
too tired to make___ it; she was too tired to fight a-bout it.

To Coda

Life in the fast__ lane, uh huh.__

Blow - in' and burn - in', blind - ed by thirst,__ they__ did-n't see the stop__ sign; took a turn__ for the worst.__ She said,

"Lis - ten, ba - by. You can hear the en - gine ring.__ We've been

AFTER THE THRILL IS GONE

Words and Music by
DON HENLEY and GLENN FREY

DOOLIN - DALTON

Words and Music by
GLENN FREY, JOHN DAVID SOUTHER,
DON HENLEY and JACKSON BROWNE

ONE OF THESE NIGHTS

Words and Music by
DON HENLEY and GLENN FREY

ON THE BORDER

Words and Music by
BERNIE LEADON, DON HENLEY
and GLENN FREY

Cruis-in' down the cen-ter of a two-way street, won-d'rin' who is real-ly in the

driv-er's seat; mind-in' my bus-'ness, a-long comes big broth-er, says

law and_ or - der, I'm try'n' to change this_ wa-ter to wine. ___

Nev-er mind your_ name, _____ just give us your num - ber, mm; _____

simile

_____ nev-er mind your face, _ just show us your card, _ mm. _

_____ And we wan-na know_____ whose wing are you un -